Stephanie Olds

The Nod

Self-Permission and the
Rise of Real Leadership

The Nod: Self-Permission and the Rise of Real Leadership by Stephanie Olds

Copyright © 2025 by Ink and Revival Publishing

Printed in the United States of America
October 2025

ISBN 978-1968178284

Ink and Revival Publishing
Virginia, USA

Table of Contents

Acknowledgements

To everyone who ever told me to wait, soften, quiet down, or shrink —thank you. You helped me discover how necessary my voice really is.

To the leaders, mentors, and colleagues who trusted my judgment before I trusted it myself — your belief helped me find my footing.

To every woman who has ever been mislabeled for her confidence, misunderstood for her clarity, or second-guessed for her presence — this book is for you. May it remind you that authority belongs to those who choose it.

To the readers walking through your own evolution of self-permission — I see you. I know the tension between humility and boldness. I wrote this so you would not have to navigate it alone.

To my family: thank you for shaping my resilience. Every chapter of my life taught me something about strength, responsibility, and identity. I carry those lessons with gratitude.

And finally, to the version of me who once waited for the nod — thank you for surviving long enough to write this book. You grew into someone you can trust.

" Authority
without humility
becomes
tyranny."

CHAPTER 1

Why We Wait

"Our deepest fear is not that we are inadequate. Our
deepest fear is that we are powerful beyond measure."
— *Marianne Williamson*

When we think about authority, many of us imagine it as something official — a badge, a promotion, a title, or the verbal blessing of someone who outranks us. But long before we enter adulthood, we are conditioned to believe that permission must come from outside of us. As children, we are trained to ask before we act, to wait before we speak, and to seek guidance before we attempt anything unfamiliar. It's a well-intentioned structure meant to keep us safe, but the unintended consequence is that we internalize dependency. We develop a belief that someone else determines when we are ready.

Those early lessons don't disappear just because we receive a job title or sign our name on an offer letter. Without realizing it, we carry the expectation into our careers. We look toward supervisors, committees, mentors, and policies to tell us when we can initiate, innovate, or decide. We become hesitant, even when our instincts are sharp and our ideas are sound. The invisible voice of childhood whispers, "Make sure you get approval first." So we wait. We wait for someone to validate what we already know.

Waiting easily becomes a habit. It can feel safe to defer decisions to someone else because shared responsibility diffuses potential blame. If we ask for permission and the outcome isn't ideal, at least we didn't act alone. That mindset is comforting to people who fear being wrong more than they value being effective. But leadership is never shaped in comfort. Great leaders emerge from the willingness to decide and then carry the outcome, whether it brings applause or consequence.

Workplace culture can reinforce this dependency in subtle ways. Many organizations unintentionally reward compliance more than leadership. Employees who act only with explicit approval are praised for caution. Those who take initiative are warned to "run it up the chain." Meanwhile, the chain often leads to someone else who is also afraid to decide without further escalation. The result is a loop of hesitation masquerading as due diligence. It's a system that nurtures title-holders, not leaders.

Underneath it all, there is often a deeper fear at work: the fear of being wrong. In school, getting a question wrong meant red ink and embarrassment. At home, making a mistake could result in discipline. At work, errors may lead to criticism or documentation. These experiences create an emotional memory that says, "Don't risk it unless someone else approves." It's no wonder so many professionals wait for certainty that no one can provide. Certainty is comforting, but authority demands courage in its absence.

There is also a social dimension to this reflex. Standing firmly in your own judgment can make others uncomfortable, especially when they haven't learned to trust themselves. When you become confident in your decisions, some people will misinterpret it as arrogance or stubbornness. Your clarity reveals their hesitation.

Your conviction highlights their doubt. The reaction you receive is not always about you; often, it's about what your confidence exposes in them.

For women — and particularly for Black women — this dynamic can be even more complicated. Cultural narratives have historically discouraged assertiveness in women, framing directness as hostility and decisiveness as aggression. Navigating authority while managing perception becomes an emotional tightrope, and many respond by diminishing themselves to keep the peace. But peacekeeping is not leadership. It is emotional labor disguised as humility.

There is a specific ache that forms when you recognize your own capability but feel tethered by unspoken expectations to stay quiet or compliant. You know you have ideas, solutions, and insight that could move a project or a team forward, yet you hesitate because you cannot point to an explicit invitation. That ache is not imagined; it's the friction of unrealized authority. It's the internal conflict between who you are now and who you were taught to be.

For many people, the turning point arrives quietly. It isn't announced, celebrated, or noticed by others. One day, something inside you grows tired of waiting for a moment that never arrives. You begin to listen to the voice that has matured through experience, struggle, resilience, and observation. You realize that you have become someone capable of deciding. That internal shift is the beginning of embodied authority. It is the moment when the voice inside becomes louder than the doubt outside.

True leadership begins with self-permission. Before you can lead teams, influence decisions, or guide strategy, you must first lead yourself. Titles can grant scope, but they cannot manufacture conviction. Real authority emerges from

> *We spend years asking for permission that no one ever had the right to give."*

the willingness to make decisions, own outcomes, and grow from the results. Leadership is not proven by perfection; it is proven by responsibility. When you carry the consequences of your choices with integrity, people trust you — not because you are always right, but because you are accountable.

Most of us don't wait because we lack ability. We wait because we've never been taught to stop waiting. We are familiar with instruction, but unfamiliar with autonomy. It's important to recognize that no one can grant you authority if you do not first grant it to yourself. You can have all the credentials, the experience, and the opportunities in the world, but if you don't trust your own voice, you will forever defer to someone else's.

If you are honest, there are likely areas of your life where you are still waiting for a nod that no one can give you. Maybe you are reluctant to propose a new idea, lead a project, start a business, or challenge a process that isn't working. Pause and name those areas. Write them down. Then ask yourself: What is the true consequence of acting without explicit permission? You might discover that the imagined consequence is far greater than the real one.

Leadership isn't measured by the number of decisions you get right; it is measured by the number of decisions you are willing to stand behind. The discomfort of responsibility is not a sign you're unqualified — it's evidence that you're growing. Once you experience the freedom of deciding from a place of self-trust, waiting for permission becomes uncomfortable in ways it never was before.

Authority is less about what you know and more about what you accept responsibility for. When you stop waiting for the nod, you begin becoming the kind of leader others can trust — not because you never fail, but because you never hide. Your authority is not something you earn in secret. It is something you step into by choice.

And once you step into it, everything changes.

Your voice steadies.
Your posture shifts.
Your decisions carry weight.
Your presence develops gravity.

Because the world responds differently to the person who has finally given themselves permission to lead.

"Leaders are not defined by the noise they make, but by the steadiness they hold."

CHAPTER 2

Titles vs. Authority

"A boss has the title. A leader has the people."
— *Simon Sinek*

Titles have become one of the most misunderstood symbols in modern leadership. We see them on email signatures, nameplates, business cards, and organizational charts. We attach weight to them because they appear to signal credibility, influence, and decision-making power. But anyone who has worked long enough inside an institution knows the truth: a title can grant you position, but it cannot manufacture authority.

Authority isn't what people call you; it's how they respond to you.

You've encountered leaders who are technically in charge, yet no one brings them problems, trusts their judgment, or seeks their guidance. You've likely also met individuals without managerial rank who have the respect, influence, and quiet gravity that draw others to them. When conflict arises or a crisis emerges, people instinctively turn toward those who carry real authority — not just the ones whose names sit higher on the chart.

This disconnect between title and authority is more common than we admit. Organizations often promote based on tenure, technical skill, or availability rather than leadership ability. The result is a structure filled with individuals who manage tasks but cannot shepherd people, who approve processes but cannot inspire action, who hold power but cannot direct momentum. When those leaders hesitate, everything slows. When they defer, direction becomes fog. When they refuse responsibility, teams feel abandoned.

At its core, authority is relational. It is built on trust, competence, consistency, and presence. A title alone may compel compliance, but only true authority inspires followership. People may obey the instructions of a title-holder, but they reserve influence for those who have earned it. Influence is a silent currency — and it's only granted to those who demonstrate they can carry the weight of decision with integrity.

Real authority also carries something titles cannot replicate: accountability. When leaders make decisions, they accept consequences. They don't hide behind committees, blame subordinates, or rely on a "sign-off" trail that transfers responsibility upward. Instead, they stand in the tension between risk and reward, knowing that leadership without accountability is merely performance.

It can be disorienting to serve under someone who doesn't embody the certainty their position implies. You might witness them pause in meetings, look around for reassurance, or defer to someone else when clarity is needed. You can feel the room's energy shift — a quiet frustration settles across the table because decision voids create emotional chaos. Teams don't know which direction to move, and uncertainty becomes the shadow that follows every project.

Contrast that with a leader who holds self-authority. When problems arise, they assess, decide, communicate, and move. They don't rush or bulldoze; they simply accept that leadership means using the information available to make a choice and adjusting if needed. Others feel safer in their presence, not because they know everything, but because they do not run from responsibility.

Interestingly, you may have already been functioning in authority long before receiving an official title. You might be the person colleagues come to for clarity,

> **"** *Position can be assigned.* *Presence must be earned."*

encouragement, troubleshooting, or advice. You might lead discussions, offer solutions, or bring calm when tension escalates. These actions reveal something: authority often emerges before it is recognized. It is visible in behavior long before it is visible in hierarchy.

Titles, on the other hand, are often reactive. Organizations award them after you've demonstrated the traits of leadership, not before. If you wait for the title to grant you validation, you're missing the point. Leadership is who you are in the absence of acknowledgment. It's the posture you carry when no one is watching, when no audience is applauding, and when no recognition is promised.

One of the more painful realizations in professional life is discovering that some people don't actually want authority; they only want the benefits of having it. They want the salary, the recognition, the quiet prestige of being "in charge," but they do not want the reality: the long hours of independent thinking, the emotional burden of uncertainty, or the vulnerability of being the one who decided. They crave the image more than the weight.

That is why authority reveals character. A person who merely wears their title will protect themselves at all costs. They will avoid blame, delay decisions, cling to approvals, and sacrifice innovation for safety. They will slow projects because they fear accountability. Meanwhile, the person with real authority will accept consequences, learn from outcomes, and adjust without losing composure.

Over time, people learn who they can trust. When the stakes get high, trust doesn't flow to the person with the highest title. It flows to the one who has demonstrated courage under pressure, emotional maturity under stress, and decisiveness when clarity is scarce. That distinction cannot be faked. It is quietly earned through repeated exposure to responsibility.

The most liberating truth you can internalize is this: You do not need a title to begin leading. You do not need permission to give your insight weight. You do not need a promotion to grow your influence. Authority is something you cultivate by showing up consistently, speaking truthfully, deciding thoughtfully, and carrying outcomes with dignity.

If you step into who you truly are, titles become confirmation — not validation.

Teams will notice. Leaders will notice. And most importantly, you will notice. Your posture changes when you stop waiting for paperwork to confirm what your character already demonstrates.

Ask yourself:

Who do people naturally follow?
Who do they confide in?
Who do they trust when direction is unclear?

Those answers are often quiet indicators of real authority at work.

Your next step is not to chase a title. It's to embody the qualities of leadership you respect — decisiveness, accountability, consistency, and presence. Because when you do, titles eventually follow. And if they don't, you will learn something even more powerful: the title you carry internally can't be stripped, overlooked, or ignored. It travels with you into every room and every opportunity.

Authority is not assigned. It is recognized.

And once you embody it, no one can take it from you.

"Permission is borrowed power — authority is internal."

CHAPTER 3

The Permission Reflex

"You become what you believe."
— *Oprah Winfrey*

Some of the most capable people you will ever meet are quietly waiting for someone else to tell them they're allowed to be who they already are. They wait for acknowledgment, direction, opportunity, or invitation, even when life has already positioned them for the work. This hesitation is rarely about talent. It is almost always rooted in conditioning.

We learn to ask for permission early, and it becomes a behavioral reflex. It shows up subtly, often without our awareness. When faced with a decision, you might feel an internal pause — a moment of uncertainty, a silent instinct that says, "Check with someone first." This pause can feel responsible, thoughtful, or collaborative. But if you observe your own patterns closely, you might discover that it's not collaboration you're seeking — it's permission.

Understanding how this reflex forms requires us to examine the systems that shaped us. Childhood teaches obedience. Schools reward compliance. Work environments measure performance against expectations set by someone else. Even well-meaning faith traditions can reinforce the belief that access to wisdom requires external authorization. These systems were designed to maintain order, not to cultivate autonomy.

As a result, many adults grow up believing that their inner voice is insufficient without external approval. This manifests in subtle ways: waiting to speak in a meeting even when you have a solution, hesitating to correct misinformation even when you're certain, or declining opportunities until someone explicitly says you're ready. We internalize the idea that we must be chosen, when the truth is that leadership begins when we choose ourselves.

Behind the desire for permission often lies a deeper fear — the fear of being wrong. Mistakes in adulthood can feel expensive, not just financially but reputationally. We worry about how we'll be perceived if our judgment misses the mark. We imagine disappointment, scrutiny, or embarrassment. But leadership is not the absence of error; it is the willingness to course-correct, learn, and continue.

The permission reflex can also be linked to identity. If you were raised in environments where your opinions were dismissed or minimized, you might have learned to distrust your own voice. If you were socialized to be agreeable, you may have internalized the belief that confidence is disruptive. If you are part of a demographic that is routinely misinterpreted, your self-assertion may have been met with discomfort or criticism. These experiences teach the nervous system to seek external validation as a form of safety.

There are workplace dynamics that amplify this reflex. Some supervisors prefer decision-making to flow exclusively through them, not because it's efficient, but because it reinforces their sense of control. Teams in these environments begin asking permission for even minor decisions, fearing reprimand if they act independently. The result is a culture where initiative quietly dies, and dependency becomes normalized.

People who live with a permission reflex often feel frustrated, not because they lack ambition, but because they sense the gap between who they are and how they show up. They feel the weight of unrealized potential. They recognize that they could do more, offer more, and contribute more if they simply trusted their judgment. That friction isn't laziness — it's a sign that your growth has outpaced your permission habits.

To break this reflex, you must learn to recognize it when it appears. Pay attention to the moments where you defer instinctively. Notice when you seek reassurance for decisions well within your competency. Ask yourself what you are afraid might happen if you act independently. You may find that the consequences you fear are remnants of an earlier version of yourself who needed more protection than you do now.

Healthy leadership posture requires that we stop outsourcing our confidence. It means accepting the burden of responsibility even when outcomes are uncertain. Waiting for someone else to endorse your decisions may protect you from criticism, but it also locks you out of growth. Authority, once embodied, demands forward motion.

It's important to differentiate between collaboration and dependency. Collaboration asks for input to deepen perspective. Dependency asks for approval to reduce fear. One strengthens your leadership; the other weakens your authority. Reflect honestly about your motivations. Are you truly seeking wisdom, or are you quietly hoping someone else will share responsibility for the outcome?

> *Silence becomes a habit long before we notice our voice went missing."*

Breaking the permission reflex also means learning to tolerate discomfort. Confidence is not built in comfort; it is cultivated through decisions that stretch your tolerance for uncertainty. Every time you choose to decide without waiting, you strengthen the internal voice that says, "You can handle this." Over time, that voice becomes familiar, authoritative, and trustworthy.

There is an emotional transformation that happens when you stop waiting to be chosen. Your language shifts from, "Can I?" to "I will." Your posture changes. You speak from a place of internal anchoring instead of external approval. People notice. Teams notice. Opportunities notice. This is how leaders emerge: not through titles, but through the courage to own their choices.

You may also notice that some people become uncomfortable when you stop asking for permission. Your independence challenges their dependency. Your clarity disrupts their comfort zone. Your decisiveness highlights their hesitation. This discomfort is not your assignment to manage. Managing others' reactions to your growth is how you shrink. Authority requires that you remain anchored, even when others are still learning to stabilize themselves.

The deeper truth is that permission was never anyone else's to give. You were waiting for something you already possessed. The nod you sought from others was an echo of the one you needed to give yourself. When you finally grant it, you begin to operate from alignment. Decisions become clearer. Boundaries become firmer. Silence becomes less frightening. You become less apologetic about existing fully in your skill, your voice, and your purpose.

The permission reflex is a scar of outdated survival. You don't have to destroy it; you only need to recognize that you've outgrown it. Let your decisions reflect the wisdom you've earned, not the fear you inherited. When you choose to lead yourself, you step into the person your younger self always hoped you would become.

The world does not change because someone gives you permission. It changes because you finally decide to show up with authority.

"Hesitation is the quiet saboteur of gifted people."

CHAPTER 4

Embodied Authority

"To handle yourself, use your head; to handle others, use your heart."
— *Eleanor Roosevelt*

Authority is not a performance; it is a posture. It doesn't arrive the day you're handed a title, nor does it disappear when others fail to recognize it. Real authority begins quietly, with internal clarity, and then takes shape through consistent behavior. It is the difference between knowing something intellectually and integrating it into the way you stand, speak, and decide.

Embodied authority is leadership lived from the inside out. It is not dependent on applause, validation, or permission. Instead, it is grounded in the awareness that you have earned the right to trust your judgment. You have stories, struggles, lessons, and scars that have shaped your discernment. When you operate from that truth, you speak with a calm confidence that does not beg to be believed.

People often misunderstand confidence as volume or dominance. But embodied authority is rarely loud. It is measured, present, and anchored. Those who carry it do not need to overexplain themselves, nor do they rush to defend every decision. Their certainty comes from a place of alignment, not ego. They are comfortable with tension because they understand that leadership includes discomfort.

When someone steps into embodied authority, others notice the shift, even if they can't articulate what changed. Meetings feel different. Conversations feel clearer. Decisions become less cloudy. There is an energetic resonance that follows people who are rooted in themselves. They don't chase approval; they attract trust.

The journey to embodied authority often begins with a private realization: you no longer need external confirmation to validate what your experience has already proven. There comes a point where you can look at the sum of your life — the challenges you overcame, the responsibilities you've held, the insight you've developed — and conclude that you are qualified to decide. This is not arrogance. It is acknowledgment.

However, stepping into embodied authority requires courage, because the moment you stop asking for permission, you become accountable for your own voice. The decisions you make will have consequences, both positive and negative. But leadership requires that you carry outcomes with the same integrity regardless of how they unfold. Authority is not the guarantee of perfection; it is the willingness to stand in the aftermath.

One of the defining traits of embodied authority is consistency. Titles can be granted overnight, but authority is built through repeated patterns of thoughtful decision-making and responsible follow-through. People trust what they see more than what they hear. Leaders who embody their authority do not change their standards depending on who is watching. They do not bend their values to win favor. They remain predictable in character, even when circumstances are unpredictable.

Embodied authority also shows up in communication. You can hear it in the way someone speaks — not rushing, not embellishing, not shrinking. They state their perspective clearly, because they have learned to trust the inner voice that guided them through harder seasons. They don't need to dominate the room; they only need to contribute with intention. Ironically, this restraint often draws more influence than force.

This kind of authority also shapes how you navigate conflict. Leaders who embody their authority do not crumble under pressure or retreat in the face of disagreement. They listen, evaluate, and respond with maturity. They don't personalize disagreement, because they understand that leadership will always invite differing opinions. Embodied authority is not brittle; it is flexible without being easily swayed.

There is an emotional grounding that comes with this posture. When you operate from embodied authority, you no longer feel threatened by feedback. You can admit when you're wrong without losing credibility, and you can stand firm when you're right without demanding validation. This emotional maturity separates leaders from title-holders. It signals that your confidence is rooted deeper than circumstance.

Interestingly, embodied authority does not seek to control others. It respects autonomy. It invites participation and insight. Leaders who are embodied do not hoard decision-making power to feel important. They share it appropriately, because they are not afraid of someone else's brilliance. Their authority is not diminished by another person's strength.

Stepping into embodied authority can feel like shedding an old version of yourself. It requires letting go of the need to be liked, applauded, or reassured. It requires trusting that your value is not dependent on external perception. For many people, this is the hardest part — not the decision-making itself, but the emotional detachment from approval.

Once you begin operating from this place, you will likely see others differently. You may notice leaders who appear confident but are actually driven by fear. You'll recognize hesitation, defensiveness, and approval-seeking more clearly than before.

Not because you are judging, but because you've outgrown those patterns. Your perspective expands when you embody the lessons you once only understood.

Another dimension of embodied authority is authenticity. You do not have to imitate anyone else's leadership style to be effective. Authority looks different on everyone. Some lead gently, others boldly. Some inspire through innovation, others through stability. The goal is not to replicate someone else's posture, but to hold your own with integrity. When your leadership aligns with your personality and values, authority flows naturally.

Authority that is not embodied feels hollow. People can sense when someone's confidence is borrowed, forced, or performative. It shows up in defensiveness, rigidity, blame-shifting, or constant need for approval. In contrast, embodied authority feels grounded. It does not demand attention; attention gravitates toward it.

As you grow, you may realize that embodied authority requires boundaries — not to keep people out, but to preserve clarity. Saying no becomes easier when you understand your priorities. Delegating becomes possible when you trust others. Pacing becomes intentional when you respect your capacity. Boundaries are not barriers; they are stewardship.

The final truth about embodied authority is simple: it cannot be faked. You can pretend to be confident, but you cannot pretend to be grounded. True embodiment is earned through experience, reflection, humility, and courage. It becomes part of how you move through the world — quietly, consistently, unapologetically.

When you reach this place, the world begins responding to you differently. Doors open. Conversations shift. Opportunities emerge. But the most important transformation is internal. You stop shrinking. You stop waiting. You become someone you trust — even when the path is unclear.

That is the essence of embodied authority: the ability to carry yourself with the weight of your own wisdom.

The moment you recognize that weight as legitimate, your leadership moves from potential to presence.

" *Authority isn't loud. It's steady.* "

"Confidence is quiet. Insecurity explains itself."

CHAPTER 5

Consequences Are Not Punishment

"The price of greatness is responsibility."
— *Winston Churchill*

One of the most misunderstood aspects of leadership is the role consequences play in growth. Many people were raised to view consequences as punishment — something handed down when we misstep, disobey, or get something wrong. That association can follow us well into adulthood, making responsibility feel threatening rather than empowering.

But leadership requires a new relationship with consequences. They are not signs of failure. They are simply the relational outcomes of decisions. Every choice — good or bad, wise or unwise — produces an effect. Those effects are not personal attacks, moral judgments, or proof of incompetence. They're information. They teach us what to adjust, reinforce what works, and refine our instincts over time.

When someone fears consequences, they often avoid decisions altogether. They defer to others, stall progress, or gather endless approvals just to ensure their fingerprints are not visible on the outcome. They believe that if they are not the one deciding, they cannot be blamed if something goes wrong. This avoidance creates a culture of hesitation and prevents leaders from developing the confidence needed to navigate uncertainty.

The truth is this: leaders cannot grow without consequences. You cannot refine your judgment if you never test it. You cannot strengthen your discernment if you only make decisions with guaranteed outcomes. Leadership includes uncertainty, and uncertainty requires courage.

It's helpful to distinguish between punishment and consequence. Punishment is about inflicting discomfort to enforce obedience. Consequence is about experiencing the natural result of an action. One is driven by control; the other is driven by accountability. When we frame every outcome as punishment, we shrink from growth. But when we view consequences as feedback, we step into maturity.

Leaders with embodied authority don't run from consequences; they accept them as proof of authenticity. They know that mistakes are a natural part of action, not a sign that they were unqualified to decide. In fact, the act of deciding — even imperfectly — is often what sets real leaders apart.

Years of experience teach us something interesting: decisions that turn out poorly are often more valuable to our leadership development than the ones that go exactly as planned. The discomfort of a misalignment becomes a teacher. It shows where assumptions were made, where context was missing, and where perspective could be improved. Leaders who embrace this learning are far more effective in the long run.

Those who fear consequences tend to operate from shame. They internalize every misstep as a reflection of their identity, rather than a reflection of a moment. They believe, "If this goes wrong, I will look incompetent." But leadership is not about never being wrong. It is about who you become after you are.

Leaders who are anchored in themselves respond to consequences without spiraling. They adjust their strategy, apologize when necessary, and communicate transparently. They do not retreat from accountability. They stand in it. That posture builds trust more than perfection ever could.

It's important to recognize how upbringing influences our perception of consequences. If mistakes in childhood were met with anger, humiliation, or harsh

> **Growth demands discomfort. Responsibility is the tuition."**

discipline, the adult nervous system may be wired to avoid risk. A simple workplace decision can trigger a fear-based response that feels disproportionate to the situation. Understanding this connection isn't about blame; it's about awareness. When you become aware of these patterns, you can work to rewrite them.

Another barrier to embracing consequences is the fear of being misunderstood. Sometimes decisions are made with integrity and wisdom, but the results are unpopular or misinterpreted. A leader must learn to tolerate discomfort in how others perceive them. Growth demands that you prioritize what is effective over what is immediately applauded. Authority becomes hollow when it is based solely on comfort.

When you step into leadership, you will sometimes make decisions that others disagree with. You will sometimes carry the weight of outcomes no one sees. You may face criticism not because you were wrong, but because you were visible. This is the cost of leadership — and visibility always carries consequence. But it also carries opportunity.

Leaders who embrace consequences develop resilience. They learn to evaluate outcomes objectively rather than emotionally. They ask, "What can I learn?" instead of, "Why did this happen to me?" This shift moves them from victimhood to agency.

They stop seeking shelter from responsibility and begin using responsibility as a tool for transformation.

There will be times when consequences are heavier than anticipated. You may endure seasons of criticism, delays, or setbacks. During those moments, remember: weight builds strength. Leadership is often defined in the moments where you refuse to collapse under pressure. Sometimes your greatest growth comes through outcomes you did not expect or desire.

Ironically, those who avoid consequences rarely avoid them for long. Deferred decisions often grow more complicated. Problems left unaddressed become heavier. Leaders who refuse responsibility eventually face consequences multiplied by delay. Authority is not found in avoidance; it is found in stewardship.

When consequences are embraced rather than feared, something powerful happens: confidence emerges. Not confidence in perfection, but confidence in recovery. You begin to trust that even if a decision doesn't go exactly as planned, you can adapt, repair, and continue. That confidence is what differentiates leaders from those who merely occupy leadership positions.

There are some outcomes that will tempt you to question your judgment entirely. You may think, "If I was a real leader, this wouldn't have happened." But growth requires reframing. Ask yourself instead, "What is this outcome teaching me about the leader I am becoming?" When you adopt this mindset, every consequence becomes an investment in your future maturity.

As you continue growing, you will encounter people who attempt to hide behind you when consequences arrive. They may look for someone to absorb blame or shield them from visibility. A wise leader recognizes the difference between offering guidance and enabling avoidance. Sharing responsibility is not the same as absorbing it for others. You must learn to let people experience the outcomes of their choices — it is the only way they grow.

Ultimately, embracing consequences is a declaration that you trust yourself enough to stand in the results of your decisions. It signals to others that your leadership is grounded, not fragile. People do not follow leaders who crumble when outcomes shift; they follow leaders who remain steady through the shift.

Consequences are not punishment. They are the teacher, the mirror, and the test. They provide clarity where theory cannot. They invite introspection where certainty fails. And over time, they turn potential into wisdom.

The leaders who leave lasting impact are not those who avoided consequences, but those who learned to carry them with integrity. When you view outcomes through the lens of growth rather than shame, you begin to lead with a quiet fearlessness. You stop shrinking from responsibility. You become the person you once waited for.

Leadership is not defined by flawless outcomes. It is defined by the courage to decide — and the character to stand afterward.

"Your presence is not a disruption. It's clarity entering the room."

CHAPTER 6

When Confidence Gets Misnamed

"If you're always trying to be normal, you will never
know how amazing you can be."
— *Maya Angelou*

A uthority is not merely about decisions and outcomes; it is also about perception. The moment you begin to stand in your authority, people respond to you based on their relationship with their own confidence—and their biases, whether conscious or not. Confidence has a complicated reputation, especially in environments where people are more comfortable with compliance than clarity.

One of the most challenging realities in leadership is that confidence does not always land as confidence. When you speak with certainty, some people interpret it as confrontation. When you advocate for boundaries or uphold standards, others may label you as difficult. These misinterpretations often have little to do with your tone and far more to do with the discomfort authority creates in those who have not developed it.

This disconnect becomes even sharper for women. Throughout history, society has rewarded women for being agreeable, adaptable, and accommodating. Directness was treated as disrespect. Assertiveness was seen as aggression. Leadership qualities that are celebrated in men are often questioned in women. The same sentence spoken by different genders can produce vastly different reactions. The message does not change—but the lens through which it is received does.

For Black women, this dynamic carries an additional layer of complexity. The intersection of race and gender creates a perception gap that can feel exhausting to navigate. Confidence becomes "attitude." Clarity becomes "tone." Boundaries become "unapproachable." Emotional neutrality becomes "angry." These labels are not rooted in your actual behavior but in the narratives that others project when confronted with authority they cannot interpret.

Many Black women learn early to shrink, soften, or over-explain to avoid triggering this response. They are taught to smile to appear less intimidating, to fold their hands to appear less assertive, to pitch their voices higher to avoid being labeled aggressive. These adjustments are not accidental; they are survival instincts formed in environments that have not evolved to recognize diverse expressions of authority.

This chapter is not about bitterness—it's about understanding. When you gain awareness of these dynamics, you stop internalizing misinterpretation as truth. You realize that perception is often a reflection of someone else's discomfort with a version of womanhood, or Black womanhood, that refuses to shrink.

Bias—especially the unconscious kind—has a way of distorting reality. Some people cannot distinguish between confidence and threat because they have been conditioned to believe that certain people should be compliant, quiet, or deferential. When you disrupt that expectation, it challenges their understanding of control. Rather than confront their bias, they rename your confidence to make it easier to categorize.

It is important to recognize that you cannot control how others receive your authority. You can only control how you embody it. If you spend your leadership energy trying to manage someone else's comfort, you will become a watered-down version of yourself. True authority cannot coexist with chronic self-shrinking.

When someone mislabels you, you have three options: internalize it, ignore it, or educate. Internalizing it drains confidence; ignoring it protects peace; educating it builds culture. Wisdom is knowing which option fits the moment. There will be spaces where your explanation is not worth the emotional labor, and others where your voice becomes a catalyst for someone else's growth.

It's also important to acknowledge that these dynamics do not only exist externally—they can quietly live within us. Sometimes, even when no one is labeling us, we fear being labeled. We hesitate because we've absorbed the possibility of misinterpretation. We silence ourselves preemptively, not because we lack confidence, but because we anticipate discomfort. This internal resistance is often more limiting than any external bias.

In professional environments, the consequences of these misinterpretations can be structural. Performance reviews may emphasize tone over results. Advancement opportunities may be shaped by perception rather than competence. Meetings may reward those who perform neutrality over those who demonstrate clarity. These dynamics create invisible barriers that many women, especially Black women, learn to navigate without a map.

Some people mislabel what they can't control."

Embodied authority gives you permission to release the burden of managing these perceptions. When you are rooted in your identity, mislabels lose their power. You begin to see them for what they are: projections. You learn to differentiate feedback from fragility. Instead of shrinking, you anchor. You speak thoughtfully, not timidly. You advocate firmly, not apologetically. You stop editing yourself to make others feel comfortable with who they have not yet become.

People who are unsure of their own authority often respond strongly to those who are sure. Your confidence will expose insecurities. Your clarity will reveal confusion. Your boundaries will unsettle those accustomed to access without accountability. These reactions are not evidence that you are wrong; they are indicators that you are growing.

There will be seasons where you question whether it's worth the emotional weight. You may feel tired of being misunderstood. You may consider shrinking just to avoid conflict. But leadership is not about comfort—it is about responsibility. When you shrink, the people watching you lose a model of what self-authorization looks like. When you stand, you expand the definition of who is allowed to lead.

One of the most powerful transformations occurs when you realize you no longer need to convince others you are not aggressive. Confidence does not need defending. Character clarifies itself over time. Let your work testify. Let your consistency speak. People may misinterpret your posture at first, but they will eventually respect what you refuse to dilute.

Authority that is rooted in identity—a clear, grounded, unapologetic sense of self— is unshakable. It does not negotiate its legitimacy. It does not beg for understanding. It does not crumble under scrutiny. The beauty of embodied authority is that it allows others to adjust their lens instead of requiring you to alter your presence.

For those who read this and recognize themselves in these paragraphs: you are not alone. Your experience is valid. Your confidence is not aggression. Your clarity is not hostility. Your boundaries are not rude. These are leadership traits, and they are necessary.

As you continue to stand in your authority, remember this truth: people who lack vocabulary for confident womanhood—and confident Black womanhood—will reach for the closest label available. Let them. Their language does not define your leadership.

Over time, your posture will educate the room.

And one day, the mislabels will no longer have power—not because they disappeared, but because you stopped shrinking to outrun them.

" Your voice
is not dangerous.
Your silence is."

CHAPTER 7

The Cost of Shrinking

"Your playing small does not serve the world."
— Nelson Mandela

There comes a point in adulthood where you begin to recognize how often you have made yourself smaller for the comfort of others. You raise your hand a little slower. You soften your voice. You take up less space in conversations. You quietly absorb tasks or responsibilities that are not yours because it feels easier than advocating for yourself. These habits are rarely conscious choices — they are survival strategies learned over years of being rewarded for compliance.

Shrinking happens gradually. It begins with one silenced thought, one deferred decision, one moment where someone else's opinion is placed above your own. You tell yourself it isn't worth the conflict to speak up. You convince yourself that someone else will lead if you don't. You decide that discomfort is a signal to retreat rather than a muscle to strengthen. Over time, these subtle concessions layer into a quieter identity. You become someone who knows but says nothing, sees but does nothing, and can but will not.

The cost of shrinking is not always visible in the moment. It shows up later — in frustration, resentment, burnout, or grief over opportunities that passed you by. It erodes your confidence because your silence becomes evidence against your capability. Every time you shrink, you reinforce a narrative that says, "My voice is optional." Eventually, you believe it.

Professional environments can unintentionally reward shrinking. Individuals who are quiet, agreeable, and unchallenging are often seen as easy to work with. They become the dependable contributors who rarely draw tension. But this praise is deceptive. It trains you to measure your value by your ability to disappear. Leaders who shrink become invisible — not because they lack talent, but because they refuse visibility.

Shrinking has emotional consequences as well. It fractures authenticity. When you are constantly editing yourself to maintain harmony, you begin to feel disconnected from your own personality. You become an observer in spaces where you were meant to participate. The more you minimize your presence, the more foreign it feels to stand fully in it.

Psychologically, shrinking conditions your nervous system to equate visibility with danger. Even neutral feedback can trigger anxiety because your identity is anchored in being unproblematic. You avoid opportunities that could elevate you because you fear the exposure. Growth becomes synonymous with threat.

There is also a spiritual cost. When you shrink, you deny the gifts you were entrusted with. You withhold your insight, your discernment, and your leadership — not because others asked you to, but because you preemptively feared their reaction. The world cannot benefit from what you bury. Potential is useless when hidden.

Identity suffers too. You cannot shrink in one area without shrinking in others. When you repeatedly silence yourself at work, you may find yourself over-explaining in relationships. When you defer leadership in professional spaces, you may over-commit in personal ones. Shrinking is never isolated. It spills.

Over time, shrinking becomes internalized as humility. But humility is not the absence of confidence — it is the presence of self-awareness. True humility recognizes your strengths accurately and uses them responsibly. Shrinking, on the other hand, distorts your self-perception. You begin to see your thoughts, ideas, and voice as less valuable than those around you.

Ironically, shrinking can create the very outcomes you fear. People may overlook you for promotions or opportunities because you appear disengaged. Your silence may be interpreted as lack of insight. Your reluctance may be read as inability. When you choose invisibility, others assume you prefer it. They cannot reward a voice they do not hear.

Another cost is relational. When you shrink to avoid intimidating others, you unintentionally teach them that your presence is negotiable. You train them to expect less from you, and worse, you teach them to give you less respect. Boundaries erode when you are not anchored in your own worth.

At some point, shrinking becomes unsustainable. You grow tired of being overlooked. You feel restless in rooms where you know you have something to contribute. You begin to feel misrepresented by the silence you chose. The internal tension becomes louder than the fear of being misunderstood.

The turning point often comes when you witness someone else embody their authority without apology. You see clarity without arrogance. You see confidence without hostility. And suddenly, you realize you could have been standing all along. This realization is painful — not because of regret, but because of recognition. You see the person you could have been if you had trusted your voice sooner.

But shame is not the answer. Awareness is. You cannot change the years you spent shrinking, but you can refuse to spend another one doing it. Once you decide to expand, you will notice resistance. Some people will struggle to adapt to your full presence because they benefited from your smaller one. Their discomfort is not a reason to return to shrinking — it is proof that you have grown.

As you step into your authority, expansion will feel uncomfortable at first. Your voice may tremble. Your body may tense. Your thoughts may race. This is not a sign that you are unqualified; it is a sign that your nervous system is unlearning old habits. The only way to normalize expansion is to practice it.

When you stop shrinking, opportunities will find you. People will ask for your insight. Teams will trust your judgment. Rooms will adjust to your presence instead of you adjusting to theirs. Leadership recognizes leadership, and expansion makes you visible to those who are searching for someone capable.

The beauty of choosing expansion is that it grants permission to others. When you take up space, you normalize it. When you speak with confidence, you model it. Someone is watching you, quietly hoping to see what leadership looks like without apology. Your expansion becomes their evidence.

The cost of shrinking is not just personal; it is generational. Every time a woman stands in her authority, the definition of leadership widens. Every time a Black woman asserts her clarity, the expectation of obedience unravels. Your voice echoes in rooms you will never enter.

When you shrink, you deprive the world of the leadership it needs. When you expand, you become the leader you spent years searching for.

Stop apologizing for your presence.

Stand fully in who you are.

Your authority is not an accident — it is the natural evolution of everything you have survived, learned, and earned.

And you were never meant to take up less space.

 Every time you shrink, you teach the room how to treat you."

"If you wait for consensus, you'll wait past your calling."

CHAPTER 8

The Nod

"When you stand in your light, you inadvertently give other
people permission to do the same."
— *Nelson Mandela (inspired)*

There comes a point in every leader's journey where something subtle but irreversible shifts. It doesn't announce itself loudly, and it rarely feels like a single dramatic moment. Instead, it unfolds like a quiet knowing — a recognition that you no longer need permission to be who you already are. This awakening is what I call *the nod*.

For much of our lives, we seek external affirmation. We want someone older, wiser, or positioned higher to acknowledge our readiness. We wait for mentors, supervisors, or institutions to validate our competence. We crave that knowing look, the verbal confirmation that says, "You're ready now." What we fail to realize is that most of the people we wait on never received such validation themselves. They simply decided.

The nod is an internal decision. It is the moment you stop performing capability and start embodying it. It's when the voice inside you becomes louder than the doubt outside you. It's when you stop rehearsing answers you already know. It's when you trust your perspective enough to speak it without apology.

Some people wait decades for *the nod*, believing it is hidden inside a promotion, a degree, or a title. They imagine that confidence will suddenly arrive once they've reached a visible milestone. But confidence doesn't descend from achievement. It emerges from alignment. You cannot wait your way into authority; you must step into it.

The moment you give yourself *the nod*, your leadership takes on a different tone. You stop second-guessing decisions you are qualified to make. You stop shrinking in rooms where your insight is needed. You stop deferring decisions out of fear of being wrong. Instead, you begin to anchor in your experience, trusting that your judgment was shaped through challenge, failure, learning, and perseverance.

Receiving *the nod* from yourself is not arrogance — it is stewardship. Arrogance assumes you are beyond growth. Authority acknowledges that growth never ends and decides anyway.

There is a spiritual element to this shift. You recognize that your gifts were not given accidentally. You acknowledge that your discernment did not develop in isolation. You understand that your voice carries weight because it was refined in seasons of silence, misunderstanding, and hard-earned clarity. When you step into that awareness, you are not elevating yourself; you are honoring the work that shaped you.

Interestingly, *the nod* is often recognized by others before you fully accept it. People come to you for advice. They trust your recommendations. They follow your lead naturally. They look to you when decisions must be made. You may not have the title, but you have the influence. Influence is the shadow of embodied authority.

But until you give yourself *the nod*, you will continue to feel like an imposter in rooms you've already earned the right to be in. Imposter syndrome doesn't reflect your lack of skill; it reflects your lack of permission. Once you stop waiting for applause, you begin performing from assurance.

You may be wondering how you know when you are ready to give yourself *the nod*. The answer is simple: readiness does not feel like certainty. It feels like responsibility. If you feel the weight of what could happen as a result of your decisions, you are already further ahead than those who lead recklessly. Real leaders are not defined by confidence alone, but by the willingness to carry outcomes with integrity.

One of the early signs of *the nod* is that you no longer feel compelled to defend every idea. Your voice steadies because your posture is anchored in more than emotional reaction. You communicate with clarity, even when others disagree. This maturity is not about winning arguments; it's about stewarding influence.

Another sign is that you stop asking for permission to be present. You enter rooms without hesitation. You offer solutions without diluting your language with "just," "maybe," or "if it's okay." You understand that your presence is not conditional — it is earned. When you speak, you no longer feel obligated to soften your expertise to protect the comfort of others.

> ❝ *The nod you're waiting for is your own.* ❞

Once you give yourself *the nod*, expectations change. You recognize that you are accountable for the voice you bring to the table. You become more intentional about what you influence, whom you empower, and how you show up. Leadership reveals character, and *the nod* summons character to the surface.

There will be moments where you doubt yourself again — that's human. New responsibilities create new insecurities. But once you have experienced the clarity that comes from internal permission, returning to silence becomes uncomfortable. Once you've expanded into your authority, shrinking no longer fits.

People may respond differently when you step fully into your authority. Some will admire your growth. Some will benefit from your clarity. Some will resist or misinterpret your confidence. Remember: their reaction is not a reflection of your readiness. It is a reflection of their relationship with self-trust.

There is, however, a responsibility embedded in *the nod*. Once you receive it, you also become someone others look to for their own permission. The most powerful leaders are those who grant others the internal courage to rise. Not by giving instructions, but by modeling what self-authority looks like in motion.

When you give yourself *the nod*, you stop auditioning. You start operating. You stop apologizing. You start contributing. You stop diminishing. You start deciding. And with each decision, your authority deepens not because you are always right, but because you always stand.

You will never feel entirely ready. You will always feel a hint of uncertainty. That is not weakness — it is stewardship. Authority without humility becomes arrogance. Humility without authority becomes hesitation. *The nod* is where the two meet.

So ask yourself: Who are you still waiting on? What approval would change anything about what you already know? Who must speak before you believe yourself?

You do not need someone else's head to tilt slightly in your direction for you to begin. You do not need applause to validate what your experience has already proven. You do not need a mentor's blessing to step into the leadership you have been quietly practicing for years.

The nod you are waiting for is your own.

And when you finally give it — fully and without apology — everything else aligns around the authority you have already earned.

" Waiting is disguise for fear."

CHAPTER 9

Qualified, Capable, Authorized

"She believed she could, so she did."
— R.S. Grey

One of the greatest internal battles leaders face is the quiet question that whispers beneath the surface: *Am I really qualified to be here?* It's a question born from comparison, reinforced by doubt, and sustained by environments that reward external credentials more than internal wisdom. But leadership — real leadership — requires that you confront and untangle this question with honesty and courage.

Qualification is not a single achievement or a line on a résumé. It is the collective sum of your lived experience, professional exposure, emotional intelligence, and personal resilience. You did not wake up qualified one morning; you became qualified through seasons that stretched you, challenged you, and demanded that you grow. Qualifications are not always visible. They are often forged quietly, long before anyone realizes you carry them.

Capability, on the other hand, reveals itself in action. It emerges each time you solve a problem no one was prepared for, offer clarity where confusion thrives, or lead with steadiness in moments others find overwhelming. Capability is not measured by how confidently you speak but by how effectively you act. It is reflected in your results, your adaptability, and your capacity to navigate complexity.

Authorization is the internal permission that completes the triad. You can be deeply qualified and undeniably capable, yet still hesitate if you do not feel authorized to use what you know. Authorization is the shift from passive potential to active leadership. It is the willingness to say, *I can do this, and I have the right to do this.* Without authorization, capability remains dormant. Without capability, qualification remains theoretical. Without qualification, authorization becomes hollow.

The truth is this: you have already demonstrated more capability than you often acknowledge. Think back to the difficult seasons of your life — the ones no one applauded, the ones where you had to navigate uncertainty without support. Those moments trained you to think clearly under pressure, to manage emotion, to interpret nuance. These are leadership competencies — not personality quirks.

Many people underestimate their qualifications because they measure themselves against the wrong standards. They compare their internal uncertainty to others' external confidence. They forget that leadership is not a performance; it is a responsibility. Those who feel unqualified often carry a deeper awareness of consequence — and that awareness makes them safer leaders.

> *Capability isn't proven by being perfect — but by standing after you aren't."*

There's a common misconception that qualification is proven through flawless execution. In reality, qualification is proven through accountable action. Leaders who refuse to move until every variable is perfect never develop the muscle of discernment. Leaders who act, reflect, adjust, and improve refine their judgment through experience. Qualification is iterative — polished through feedback, not perfection.

It's important to recognize how imposter syndrome disguises itself. It does not simply tell you that you are unqualified. Sometimes, it tells you that you should wait until conditions are ideal. It tells you to gather just a bit more experience, earn one more certification, or receive one more endorsement. In truth, imposter syndrome thrives on delay. It convinces you that someday will be safer than today. Leadership rejects that myth. It asks you to decide with what you know, trusting that what you learn next will refine you further.

Authorization becomes especially critical for women — and even more so for Black women — because societal norms have historically questioned our readiness. When culture tells you that you are aggressive instead of assertive, emotional instead of passionate, or intimidating instead of confident, you begin to internalize the idea that your authority must be justified. Authorization disrupts that narrative. It allows you to stand without apology, to speak without shrinking, and to lead without asking permission to exist in your power.

At some point in your journey, responsibility becomes the greatest indicator of qualification. If others trust you during critical moments, if they seek your judgment when stakes are high, if opportunities find you even before titles do, understand this: people do not gravitate to incompetence. They gravitate to presence. Trust is an external recognition of internal qualification.

To deepen your sense of self-authority, consider these three questions:

1. What have I already overcome that someone else is still trying to figure out? Resilience is a credential.

2. What do people consistently come to me for?

Patterns reveal competency.

3. What challenges have I navigated without instruction?

Independence reveals capability.

When you reflect honestly, you begin to see that qualification is not a badge granted by hierarchy. It is a reality demonstrated by your history.

Of course, capability is not static. True authority requires ongoing growth. Leaders who believe they have learned everything stop deserving what they have been given. Capability expands through curiosity, feedback, and humility. Authorization is not a declaration that you have arrived; it is a commitment to continue maturing.

Authority also requires boundaries. When you are qualified and capable, people will pull on your time, your emotional bandwidth, and your expertise. They will ask you to solve problems they avoided, carry tasks they neglected, or make decisions they fear. Boundaries protect your capacity. They prevent burnout. They preserve energy for the responsibilities that truly align with your purpose. Authorization without boundaries becomes exploitation.

One of the most powerful identity shifts you can make is moving from *I hope I can* to *I know I can*. This shift does not negate humility. It simply honors reality. When you trust your preparation — not perfection, but preparation — you lead with steadiness. When you trust your instincts — not impulsively, but intentionally — you move with clarity. When you trust your presence — not loudly, but confidently — you influence without force.

You will encounter environments that question your readiness, not because you are unqualified, but because your authority disrupts familiarity. Do not mistake resistance for deficiency. Sometimes others see your capability before you do. Their discomfort becomes confirmation.

There is one more truth that leaders must internalize: authorization is not earned once; it is reaffirmed repeatedly. Every new challenge will ask, *Are you still standing in your authority?* Every new level of responsibility will stir uncertainty. Growth will always invite a fresh decision to believe in yourself.

But each time you choose your voice, each time you decide without shrinking, each time you stand in the aftermath of a difficult outcome, you reinforce the foundation of your authority. Leadership becomes less about proving yourself and more about being yourself.

You are qualified because you have done the work that life demanded of you. You are capable because you carry the wisdom that experience shaped in you. You are authorized because you decided to stop waiting for someone else to validate what your journey already confirmed.

The world needs leaders who understand all three.

" Leaders are not defined by the noise they make, but by the steadiness they hold."

CHAPTER 10

Leading Forward

"As we are liberated from our fear, our presence automatically liberates others."
— *Marianne Williamson*

Leadership evolves the moment it extends beyond the self. Internal authority is the foundation, but its purpose is not isolation — it's impact. Once you begin trusting your own voice, owning your decisions, and embodying your authority, the question becomes: *What will you do with it?* Leading forward means transforming your growth into something others can experience, learn from, and build with.

Leadership is not merely about directing others. It is about shaping environments, stewarding influence, and modeling a way of being that invites others to rise. When you stop waiting for permission, you create space for others to do the same. Your courage becomes contagious. Your clarity becomes stabilizing. Your standards become instructional. Authority does not end with you; it travels through you.

Leading forward requires awareness. Not everyone will celebrate your growth. Some will resist it. Others may misunderstand it. When you stop shrinking, you disrupt dynamics that depended on your silence. But leadership does not bend to accommodate comfort — it challenges comfort to accommodate growth. Navigating this tension is part of the responsibility you carry.

One of the first shifts you'll notice when you lead forward is how intentionally you begin to make decisions. You think not only about immediate outcomes but about the ripple effect of your choices. You consider how your actions influence culture, how your tone affects morale, and how your posture shapes expectation. Authority teaches you that leadership is not about control; it is about stewardship.

Stewardship sees beyond the moment. It recognizes that your position is temporary but your impact is not. Titles expire. Influence does not. When you lead forward, you invest in clarity, communication, and accountability because you know these are the threads that hold teams together when uncertainty threatens morale.

The leaders who leave lasting impressions are not the ones who hoard opportunity — they are the ones who cultivate it in others. They pay attention to who is overlooked and invite them into visibility. They listen for voices that tremble and offer development instead of critique. They mentor without requiring imitation. Leading forward demands that you see potential in others even before they see it in themselves.

However, leading forward does not mean carrying everyone. It means discerning who is willing to carry themselves. A leader who tries to rescue everyone eventually becomes ineffective. Your responsibility is to model, guide, correct, and expect. You cannot want growth more for someone else than they want it for themselves. Authority without boundaries becomes exhaustion.

Clarity is one of the most powerful tools of forward leadership. People cannot follow direction they do not understand. When you communicate expectations clearly, you create psychological safety. When you articulate purpose, you offer meaning. When you provide context, you empower decision-making. The clearer you are, the stronger your teams become.

Another dimension of leading forward is emotional maturity. You will encounter disagreement. You will make decisions that others don't appreciate. You will be misunderstood by people who do not have access to your reasoning. Your ability to remain anchored through critique is what separates real leadership from performance. Feedback should refine you, not define you.

Forward leadership also demands accountability. Accountability without shame strengthens culture. It teaches that mistakes are opportunities, not indictments. When consequences are embraced instead of avoided, trust deepens. People learn that leadership is not about being right, but about being responsible. When your team sees you own outcomes — especially difficult ones — they learn to do the same.

One of the most overlooked aspects of leadership is pacing. Not every moment requires urgency. Forward leadership understands when to push and when to pause. Sometimes the most effective decision is not acceleration, but alignment. Leaders who are constantly hurried produce exhausted teams. Leaders who pace intentionally produce sustainable growth.

Leading forward means confronting fear. Not just your own — but others' fear of change, fear of failure, and fear of visibility. Growth demands discomfort. When you normalize discomfort, you remove the stigma associated with development. Your example helps others reframe fear as a teacher instead of a threat.

You will also discover that forward leadership is often quiet. It is not always celebrated. It is not always visible. Sometimes it looks like staying late to think through a problem others quit too early to solve. Sometimes it means having difficult conversations others avoid. Sometimes it means making decisions that will not be understood for months. Leadership is not glamorous; it is grounded.

There will be seasons where forward leadership feels lonely. Not because you are unsupported, but because you are responsible. While others may complain, you must stay composed. While others may seek comfort, you must pursue clarity. While others may resist growth, you must model it. Loneliness is not evidence you are wrong; it is evidence you are leading.

However, forward leadership is not meant to be isolating. It thrives in community with others who carry similar weight. Seek mentors who challenge you. Seek peers who sharpen you. Seek environments that stretch you. Isolation creates stagnation; alignment creates evolution.

As you continue to lead, you will notice that your authority begins to shift from positional to relational. People follow you not because they have to, but because they trust you. Trust is the currency of sustainable leadership. It cannot be demanded. It is earned slowly and lost quickly. Protect it.

> *Legacy begins the moment you stop leading for applause and start leading for impact."*

Forward leadership also includes succession. The mark of true authority is not how many people you outrank, but how many leaders you develop behind you. Legacy is not measured by accolades; it is measured by continuity. The leadership you build must outlast your presence.

To lead forward is to accept that your decisions contribute to a narrative larger than yourself. You are building culture — even when you think you are only completing tasks. You are shaping expectations — even when you believe you are only sharing feedback. Culture is formed in the moments leaders assume go unnoticed.

As you prepare for the chapters of leadership ahead, anchor yourself in three realities:

You are accountable for your posture.

Authority without humility becomes tyranny.

You are accountable for your influence.

Silence and speech both teach.

You are accountable for your integrity.

Character is leadership's foundation — without it, nothing stands.

Leading forward is not the final step of authority; it is its expression. It is where internal alignment becomes external transformation. It is where decisions evolve into direction, where clarity becomes culture, and where presence becomes legacy.

Leadership is not something you have. It is something you embody — every day, in every room, through every decision.

And when you lead forward, you show others what it looks like to walk boldly without waiting, to stand firmly without shrinking, and to move confidently without permission.

Your authority was not an accident.

Your capability was not incidental.

Your voice was not a coincidence.

Lead forward — because someone is watching, hoping, and learning how to rise.

" Authority is stewardship, not spotlight."

CONCLUSION

The Moment You Decide

"Once you make a decision, the universe conspires to make it happen."
— Ralph Waldo Emerson

Authority is not earned in a single breakthrough. It is built in layers — through seasons of doubt, through hard-won lessons, through the quiet courage of choosing yourself when others hesitated. You arrived here not because someone appointed you, but because you continued to rise, even when permission was absent.

If there is one truth this book has woven into your leadership DNA, it is this: **No one can authorize your voice but you.**

Titles may recognize your ability, systems may benefit from your competence, and teams may rely on your presence — but none of these external affirmations mean anything until you internalize them. Authority without self-acceptance is fragile. Authority without responsibility is dangerous. Authority without embodiment is hollow.

You already carry everything necessary to lead forward.

Not perfectly — but faithfully.

Not without fear — but without surrender.

There will always be reasons to wait. There will always be voices that prefer your silence. There will always be systems more comfortable with compliance than clarity. But leadership asks something of you that waiting never will: courage.

Courage to decide when the outcome isn't guaranteed.

Courage to speak when silence would be easier.

Courage to stand fully in who you are, even when others have not yet learned how to receive it.

The world does not need more positional leaders. It needs more anchored ones. Leaders who understand that authority is stewardship, not dominance. Leaders who carry conviction without aggression, clarity without arrogance, presence without apology.

As you move forward, remember that authority is a discipline. You must choose it daily. Every decision you make either reinforces your voice or diminishes it. When uncertainty surfaces — and it will — anchor yourself in the truth that your judgment has been shaped through experience, resilience, and reflection. You are not deciding blindly; you are deciding based on everything life has already taught you.

Your existence in leadership spaces is not accidental. Your clarity is not threatening — it's necessary. Your boundaries are not rude — they're responsible. Your confidence is not aggression — it's authority. Stop diluting your potential to preserve someone else's comfort.

Leaders do not serve the room by shrinking.

You serve the room by showing up whole.

So this is your charge:

Decide even when the outcome is unclear.
Stand even when perception is skewed.
Speak even when misunderstanding is possible.
Lead even when approval is absent.

You are qualified.
You are capable.
You are authorized.

Leadership is not a destination.
It is a becoming.

And you — bold, intentional, grounded — are already on your way.

Lead forward.
Without apology.
Without hesitation.
Without fear.

Your nod has already been given.

Now go.

Reflection Questions

Use these to deepen your awareness and align your leadership posture:

Identity

1. In what areas of your life do you still seek external approval to validate internal truth?
2. What beliefs about yourself must you release to step fully into your authority?

Authority

3. Where are you shrinking to preserve someone else's comfort?
4. What decision are you avoiding because you fear the consequence more than the stagnation?

Responsibility

5. How do you respond when outcomes are imperfect? What does that say about your leadership maturity?
6. What boundaries do you need to set to protect your capacity and integrity?

Perception

7. How have mislabels or biased interpretations shaped your voice, tone, or presence?
8. Who benefits when you shrink, and who suffers when you do?

Legacy

9. What example are you modeling for those watching you — silently hoping to see courage?
10. What impact do you want your authority to create beyond your title, role, or season?

Take your time. Answer honestly. Your responses are the blueprint for your next level.

Notes

Notes

Notes

Notes

Notes

Notes

Notes